Mill Life
at
STYAL

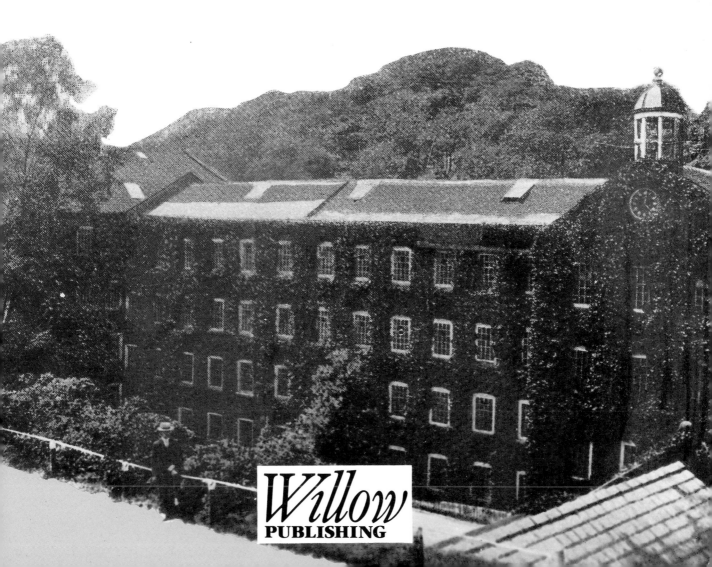

Willow
PUBLISHING

Contents

Willow Publishing
Willow Cottage, 36 Moss Lane,
Timperley, Altrincham,
Cheshire, WA15 6SZ.

©Quarry Bank Mill Trust 1986

ISBN 0 946361 19 3

Printed by The Commercial
Centre Ltd., Clowes Street,
Hollinwood, Oldham.

Acknowledgements

*For permission to reproduce photographs we are grateful to the
following: BBC Hulton Picture Library: satirical cartoon Pg 40,
cotton operatives rioting Pg 42. British Library: Albion Mills Pg 32.
ILN Picture Library: Manchester Dwellings Pg 17, Raiding the
Workhouse, Stockport Pg 40. Manchester Public Libraries, Local
History Library: The Factory Girl Pg 36. Mansell Collection: Slums
1852, Pg 15. Viscount Knutsford of Munden, Watford, Herts:
Portrait of Dr Holland Pg 30. Bedworth Woollen Mill reproduced by
permission of Lord Daventry Pg 34. Boy sweeping Pg 23, Crown
copyright.*

Other illustrations are from the Quarry Bank Mill Archives.

Introduction

In October 1984, the year of its bicentenary, Quarry Bank Mill opened its doors to a select group of visitors. The Mill's guests on this day were descendants of Styal's workforce of generations past. The Mill's curatorial staff met many family groups and were shown a fascinating array of family photographs, documents and artefacts all relating to the families experiences at Quarry Bank Mill. This was one event in a twelve month programme which aimed to research the world of the Mill Worker at Styal.

The information gleaned has been presented in Styal's Social History Gallery, The Mill Workers' World. The text is reproduced here.

The display forms an integral part of exhibitions showing work at the Mill. A working weaving shed and a mule spinning room illustrate actual working conditions.

A major part of the exhibition is a reproduction of a Mill Worker's cottage. Great attention has been paid to detail, each feature being reproduced from an examination of cottage properties in the village of Styal. These cottages are occupied and therefore unavailable to the general visitor. The Mill is grateful to Vincent Shawcross and Steve Jones for their work on this project.

The research, design and exhibition work for the Mill Workers' World project was carried out by the Mill's Curator, Nigel Nixon, Josselin Hill and a team of Manpower Service personnel.

Many historic photographs came to light during the research process. Some of these have been reproduced in the gallery.

The Mill is grateful to Ilford (UK) for their support, and in particular to Mike Waldron and his team for the great care and skill shown in their patient reproduction of faded historic photographs.

For their help with this project the Mill would also like to thank the North West Museum and Art Gallery Service and Mack of Manchester.

Oak Cottages c.1890.

Situated south of Manchester, Styal Village is a remarkable example of a surviving factory community which developed to supply the workforce of nearby Quarry Bank Mill.

It was built by Samuel Greg in 1784 as a water powered cotton spinning mill, then given to the National Trust in 1939 by Alec Greg his great, great grandson.

The village has been restored and the mill is being developed by a separate charitable trust as a working museum of the cotton industry.

Mill Girls c.1920

'The Millworkers' World'

How did it compare to life in the towns?

Samuel Greg built Quarry Bank near the hamlet of Styal. It was sited on the River Bollin where a fall in the river's course provided a potential source of power.

He also needed a workforce. His son, Samuel Junior, later wrote on the best way to recruit and keep loyal and reliable workers:

'Fair wages; comfortable houses; gardens for their vegetables and flowers; schools and other means of improvement for their children; sundry little accommodations and conveniences in the mill, and interest in their general welfare.'

Other members of the family appear to have shared his views.

The Factory Debate

In the 19th century a great debate took place on whether factory life was harmful to society and to the men and women who operated the machines.

Robert Hyde Greg, second master of Quarry Bank Mill, argues that **'most of the evils of great factories are the evils of great towns'**.

The environment of the factory was all important. In his book *The Factory Question* (1833) he compared the squalor of the crowded towns to the pleasant rural setting of Styal. Others argued that it was the factory system itself that was at fault.

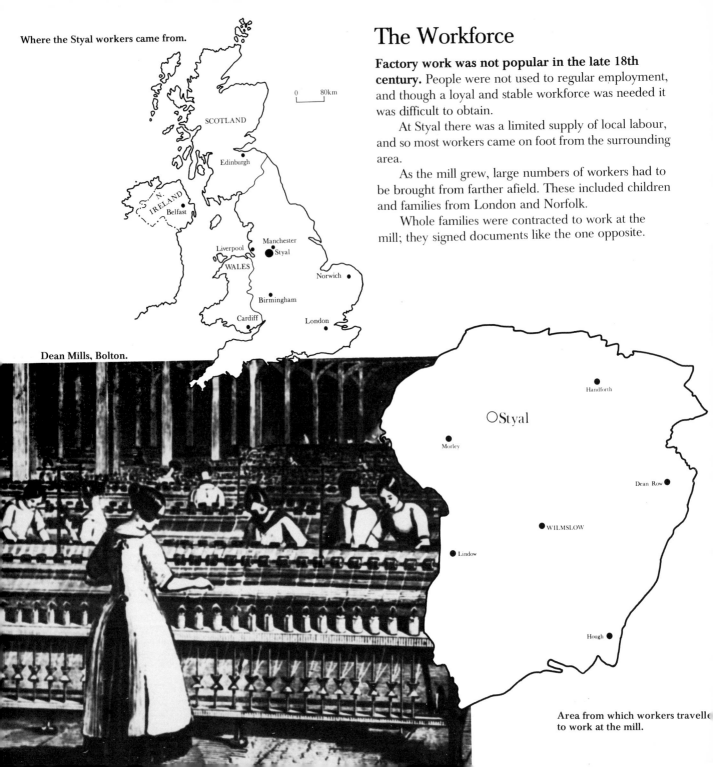

0   80km

SCOTLAND

Edinburgh

N.
IRELAND
Belfast

Liverpool   Manchester
            ● Styal
WALES

Norwich

Birmingham

Cardiff   London

Dean Mills, Bolton.

The Workforce

Factory work was not popular in the late 18th century. People were not used to regular employment, and though a loyal and stable workforce was needed it was difficult to obtain.

At Styal there was a limited supply of local labour, and so most workers came on foot from the surrounding area.

As the mill grew, large numbers of workers had to be brought from farther afield. These included children and families from London and Norfolk.

Whole families were contracted to work at the mill; they signed documents like the one opposite.

Handforth

○Styal

Morley

Dean Row ●

● WILMSLOW

● Lindow

Hough ●

Area from which workers travelle to work at the mill.

Be it remembered, it is this Day agreed by and between ROBERT HYDE GREG, JOHN GREG, and SAMUEL GREG, of Styal, in the County of Chester, of the one Part, and *John Stevens, on behalf of himself and his four children, Elizabeth Stevens, Rebekah Stevens, James Stevens and Mary Stevens of Styall in the County of Chester* of the other Part, as follows: That the said *John Stevens and his four children* shall serve the said ROBERT HYDE GREG, JOHN GREG, and SAMUEL GREG, in their Cotton-Mills, in Styal, in the County of Chester, as just and honest Servants *John 12 & his children 11* Hours in each of the six working Days, and to be at *their* own Liberty at all other times; the commencement of the Hours to be fixed from Time to Time by the said ROBERT HYDE GREG, JOHN GREG, and SAMUEL GREG, for the term of *Two* Years at the Wages of *Twenty Six Shillings per week for the first year and Twenty nine Shillings per week for the second year*

AND if the said *John Stevens or any of his four children* shall absent *themselves* from the Service of the said ROBERT HYDE GREG, JOHN GREG, and SAMUEL GREG, in the said working Hours, during the said Term, without their consent first obtained, that the said ROBERT HYDE GREG, JOHN GREG, and SAMUEL GREG, may abate the Wages in a double proportion for such absence; and the said ROBERT HYDE GREG, JOHN GREG, and SAMUEL GREG, shall be at Liberty, during the Term, to discharge the said *John Stevens and his four children or each of them* from their Service, for Misbehaviour, or Want of Employ.

As Witness their Hands, this *Third* Day of *February* 1835

Robert Hyde Greg

Witness

Philip Henry Fletcher

John his X *Stevens* mark

Family contract dated 1835.

The Venables family at Styal

Members of the Venables family have worked at Quarry Bank Mill since 1790. This family tree identifies them: several are referred to in other sections.

The man pictured with his wife, *right* is Thomas Venables, who worked as a mechanic at the mill. His great-grandfather George, starting as an apprentice in 1790, was the first Venables to work here. He settled in the village and had a large family.

In November 1984, descendants of Styal workers were invited to the mill. The picture *below right,* taken on that occasion, shows members of the Venables family today. Alice Maud, who is the great-great-granddaughter of George Venables, still lives locally.

Thomas Venables and his wife Elizabeth Ann Worth.

Jane Venables nee Jackson.

Robert Venables
b 1745
m Abigail Jones

Robert	**George**	and four
b 1777	1779–1830	others
	m Mary Moss	
	b 1780–1836	

John	**Robert**	**George**	and eight
1806–72	1816–76	*b* 1822	others
m (i) Hannah Henshaw			
1806–65			
(ii) Mary Ann Oakes			
b 1818			

John	**Hannah Mary**	and seven
1834–65	*b* 1836	others
m Jane Jackson		
b 1838		

Thomas	and one
b 1863	other
m Elizabeth Ann Worth	

| **Alice Maud** | and three |
| *b* 1898 | others |

Thomas Venables and Family.

In the Mill ...
jobs and duties

The Mill Owner

↓

The Mill Manager

↓

Engineers and mechanics looked after the machinery and the Steam Engine.

In charge of each room were **Overlookers.**

Clerks worked in the mill office.

Preparing the raw cotton

Mixers
the men, women and sometimes children who blended the raw cotton fibres together.

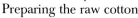

Carders
men who worked the machines that straightened the cotton fibres. Women **Tenters** helped them. **Doffers** were children who took the fibres to the next process.

Drawers and Rovers
women and children in charge of the machine that drew out the cotton and added a loose twist.

Bobbin winders
children who wound the spun thread onto bobbins for the creel frame.

Spinning

Throstle spinners
women and children who worked on Arkwright's water frame or *throstles*, which produced a strong warp thread.

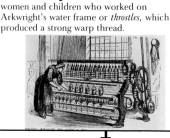

Mule spinners
men and women who spun on Crompton's Mule, which produced a finer thread. They were helped by **Piecers** who twisted the threads together when they broke.

Weaving

Warpers/Beamers
men and women who prepared the warp for the loom by winding it onto a beam from a creel frame.

Drawers
men and women who drew the warp threads through the 'eyes' and 'dents' of the harness making them evenly spaced, ready for weaving. Tacklers then placed the prepared warp in the loom frame.

*Tacklers** then put the prepared warp in the loom frame.

Weavers
men and women who operated the looms helped by child **Tenters.**

Average weekly wages

		Manchester	Styal
1833	Children under 13	3/9d to 4/2d	1/- to 3/-
1833–50	Reelers and winders	8/- to 9/6d	4/- to 7/-
1834–50	Carding (male adults)	13/6d to 16/-	8/- to 17/-
1834–50	Carding (female adults)	8/-	6/6d to 7/-
1838–50	Mule spinners (male)	16/- to 22/-	10/- to 13/-
1838–50	Throstle spinners (female)	7/6d to 10/6d	6/- to 7/-
1846–50	Weavers (male and female)	10/6d to 11/-	6/6d to 8/-

Robert Venables' first house in Styal, at Farm Fold.

Wages

In the Cotton Industry most workers earned fixed wages; but spinners were paid piece rates so that when there was a slump in trade wages would be reduced.

The wages paid at Quarry Bank Mill were lower than those paid at Manchester and Stockport but the standard of living of the workforce could well have been higher.

Women were generally paid less than men. It is interesting to compare wages paid at Quarry Bank Mill with those commanded by other occupations . . .

Average weekly wages
at Quarry Bank Mill
1831

Male Carders 17/- to 18/-
Female Spinners 6/6d
Reelers 5/- to 10/-
Mechanics 18/- to 22/-

Average weekly wages
in Manchester
1832

Shoemakers 15/- to 16/-
Carpenters 24/-
Tailors 18/-
Labourers 12/-

Robert Venables 1816–1876

Good workers could expect promotion to different and more responsible jobs. As a hand was promoted, his name moved up the list of workers for each shed in the wages book.

George Venables, having started as an apprentice, later became an engineer. His son Robert's career can also be followed:

1834–36 Listed as working in 1st Carding Room.

By **1839** had risen to take charge of the 3rd Weaving Room with a total of 14 hands beneath him.

1841 Promoted to second-in-charge of 2nd Weaving Room containing 45 hands.

By **1847** had taken charge of the 5th Weaving Room with 35 hands.

1848 Moved from original home at No. 7 Farm Fold Cottages to 5 Acre Farm on Moss Lane, employing a farm hand.

1869 Farm now 7 acres.

1870 Robert retired after continuing to work as Overlooker as well as maintaining the farm.

By **1871** the farm encompassed 19 acres.

The building of Styal

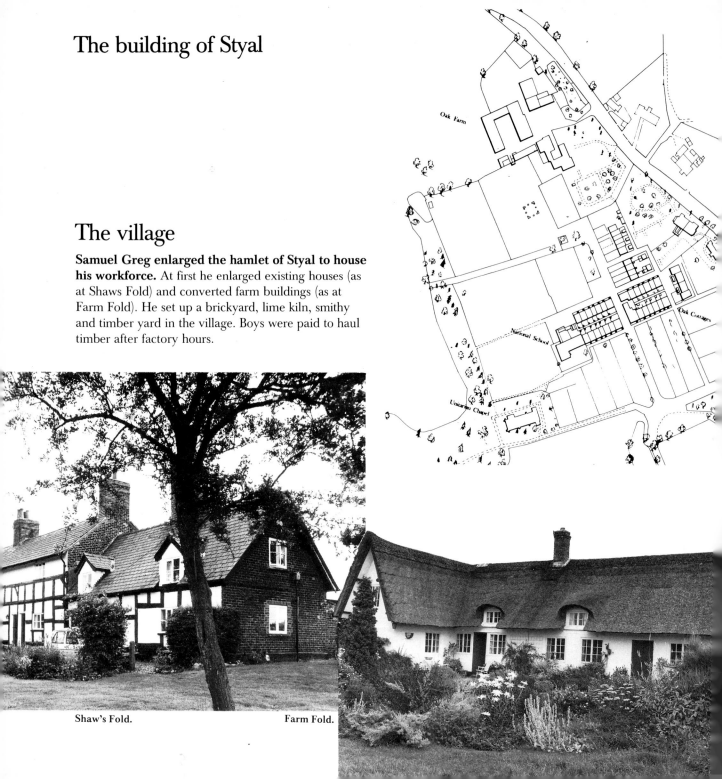

The village

Samuel Greg enlarged the hamlet of Styal to house his workforce. At first he enlarged existing houses (as at Shaws Fold) and converted farm buildings (as at Farm Fold). He set up a brickyard, lime kiln, smithy and timber yard in the village. Boys were paid to haul timber after factory hours.

Oak Farm

Oak Cottages

National School

Unitarian Chapel

Shaw's Fold.

Farm Fold.

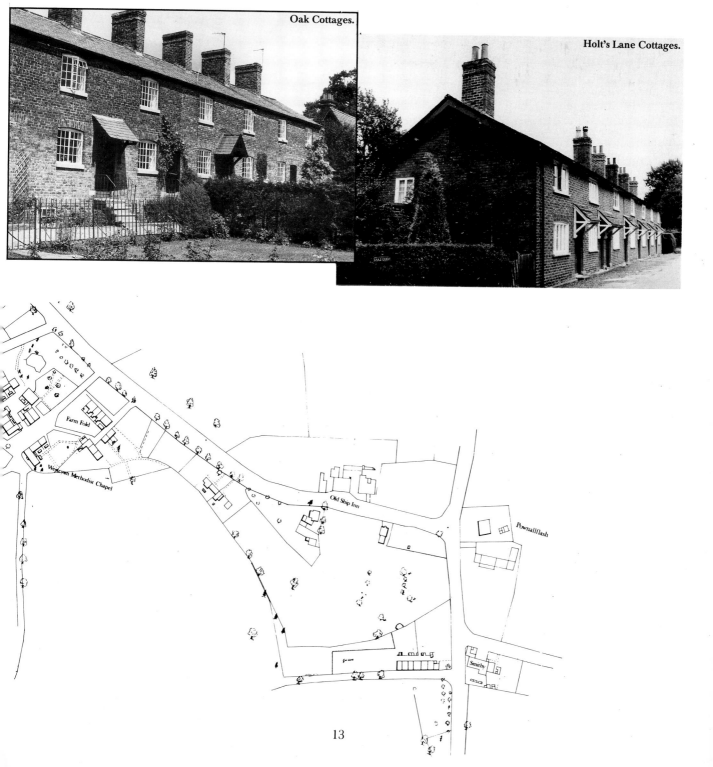

Oak Cottages.

Holt's Lane Cottages.

Farm Fold

Wesleyan Methodist Chapel

Old Ship Inn

Pownallflash

Smithy

13

New housing

'The houses in Styal are commodious, clean, whitewashed and in every respect superior to the habitations for a similar class of labourers in the town . . . (which) are filthy.' P GASKELL, 1836

The houses that Samuel Greg built at Styal were similar to those built in the towns. In Styal, villagers had the natural benefit of rural surroundings; in overcrowded towns, with inadequate sanitation, such houses quickly became slums. Styal's houses were separated by courts and alleys; 'back-to-back' type houses were never built here.

Oak Cottages

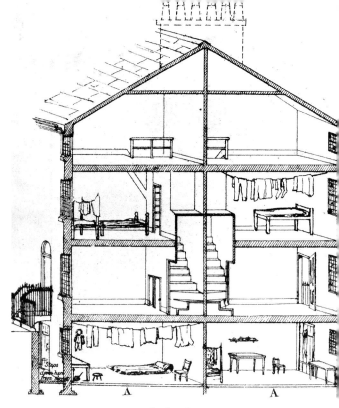

Back-to-back houses in Manchester.

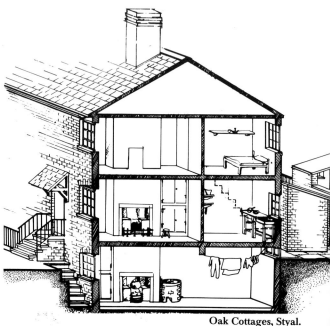

Oak Cottages, Styal.

14

Country and Town

At Styal each cottage had its own allotment, and every house had a privy. In the town as many as one hundred people had to share a privy. Many of the houses were totally undrained, and stagnant waste piled up around them.

'The population (in Manchester) is crowded into one dense mass of cottages separated by unpaved and almost pestilential streets. This is an atmosphere loaded with the exhalation of a large manufacturing city.' J P KAY, 1832

Manchester slums, 1852.

A COURT FOR KING CHOLERA.

Cottages.

Tenements by the Irwell.

Rents

Rents paid at Styal were lower than in the towns as they were based on agricultural rates. Varying from 1/- to 2/6d, they were deducted from workers' wages. In contrast, the rent paid by John Prince, a spinner of Manchester, in 1830 averaged 3/7d a week.

Records show that an average of eight people lived in each cottage in Styal (1844–53).

The cellars were rented separately, usually to widows. Originally, the cellars may have been intended as loomshops. Some were used for this purpose. It is possible that Samuel Greg saw Quarry Bank as a self-contained operation: spinning in the factory and weaving in the home. The development of the power loom would have made this impractical.

Unlike those in Styal, the cellars in urban slums were rented out to large numbers of the poorest people, so overcrowding was common.

Overcrowded urban cellar, 1850.

An Oak Cottage cellar today.

Goods and chattels

'The houses of great numbers of the labouring community in the manufacturing districts present many traces of the savage life ... what little furniture is found in them is of the rudest and most common sort ....' P GASKELL, 1833

Engravings of Manchester tenements in the 1850s would seem to support this view.

The workers had very few furnishings and possessions. The mortgage of William Chadwick of Styal, 1794, provides an inventory.

The contents of a Manchester tenement in the 1840s had changed little from the contents of William Chadwick's cottage at Styal 50 years earlier.

Utensils	Furnishings	Ornaments
Box	Strips of mat/and faded carpet	Glazed tea-tray
Meal or flour barrel	Deal table	Small prints in black frames
Smoke-browned chintz	Chairs	Metallic 8-day Dutch clock with pendulum
Plates	Stools	Stoneware ornaments
Dishes	Settles	Geraniums
Dinner service	Small mahogany table	
Cooking implements	Small sofa	
	Cradle	
	Large cupboard	
	Muslin window screen	
	Cotton curtains	

(List derived from A. Bethune Reach, *Manchester and the Textile Districts in 1849*)

Manchester Dwellings 1862.

MORTGAGE IN CHATTELS

Styall
28th Day of Octor 1794

By this Indenture I bind myself to pay unto Mathw Fawkner of Styall the sum of five pounds Eleven shillings upon Demand and also Asign Over my Household goods under mentioned unto the aforesaid Mathw Fawkner till the aforesaid sum of five pounds 11s. is paid and also allow him to sell them or any part of them for the Payment of the aforesaid money and all Expenses attending such sale of my goods.

William Chadwick

One Chest	14/–	Shaffill	1/–
One Iron Pot	2/–	Hatchet	2/–
One Clock	21/–	Rugs	2/6
1 Bed Stocks	9/–	Tin Kettle	1/–
1 do ∞	—	Potts and Mugs	5/–
7 Chairs	12/–	Cupboard	8/–
Bellis	2/–	Map	2/6
1 Pair Bed Stocks	2/6	Little Stand	1/9
Iron and Heater	5/6	Iron Pott	5/–
3 Glass Pictures (small)	6d	Sheets	8/–
One Map	1/8	Blankets	10/–
Table	6/–	Copper Kettel	2/6
One Stand	1/6	Sundry Things	1/4
Grate and Tongs	11/6		
Frying Pann	1/4		
Bed Clothes	28/–		
Fork	1/11		
Spade	1/4		

William Chadwick

Styal Village Shop.

Standard of living

In general the standard of living at Styal was better than that experienced in the towns.

Although wages paid in Manchester were higher than (or at least comparable to) those paid in Styal, the Styal workforce was better off because in an agricultural area, fresh food was cheaper, and also the cottage allotments enabled families to grow some of their own food.

The Village Shop

In the 1820s a shop was opened in the village. It stocked the staple foods of factory workers all over England: flour, meal, potatoes, and bacon. Houshold goods, clothing and millinery were also sold; a tailor visited the shop to fit customers. Thrifty villagers raised livestock which they sold to the shop: John Venables sold a pig in 1836.

The shop at Styal was run on a co-operative system. so that the profits could be shared. The Gregs also enjoyed interest on the money they invested. In the 1820s the shop made an annual profit of about £150 on sales of around £1,700.

A shilling spent on fresh food in Styal would probably have bought more than a shilling spent in an urban area like Bolton or Manchester.

Plan of the allotments near Oak Cottages.

The Truck System

The shop was run on the **truck** system: the cost of whatever the workers bought was automatically deducted from their wages.

   This was because there was a shortage of coinage and it was easier for money to change hands only in the pages of an account book. In many mills, workers were forced to use shops run by the mill owners. In some mills 'tokens' replaced Royal Mint coinage. In many mills, 'truck' was abused and mill owners profited at the expense of their workers; poor quality or adulterated goods were sold at high prices.

Common types of food adulteration
Tea leaves were redried and retinted for resale; iron filings were added to increase weight.
Sugar was weighted with sand and dirt.
Beer had salt added to increase thirst, sulphuric acid to improve flavour, and tobacco for colouring.
Cider wine had lead added for flavour.
Flour was weighted with alum, chalk or pipe clay.
Milk was watered down with added chalk and flour.
Bread had mashed potato, alum or copper sulphate added.

There is no evidence that such abuses existed in Styal.
   In 1833, a mechanic would have had to work an average of 3 hours to earn enough to buy the goods shown *(below)*. (These prices were recorded in Bolton that year.)
   In 1985, a factory worker earning £5,500 a year would have to work 2 hours for the same goods.

1 lb **flour** 2d, 1 lb **potatoes** ½d, 1 lb **butter** 3d, 1 quart **milk** 2d, 1 lb **bread** 1½d, 1 lb **beef** 1½d.

Apprentices

Two brothers George and Robert Venables, were sent to Quarry Bank Mill from the Parish of Whitchurch in 1790. They were then aged 11 and 13. As with the Gregs' other child apprentices, they worked a period of probation and were then bound by an apprentice indenture.

This committed them to work for a certain number of years at the mill in return for food, clothes, lodging, and a very small wage in return for overtime. *'Apprenticeship' no longer meant a period of training leading to a trade as in the Middle Ages.*

Mill owners like Samuel Greg relied heavily on apprentice labour because, in the 1790s they were inexpensive to keep; they were nimble-fingered and physically suited for the work; a young person was easy to train to do simple tasks, and many were available when local labour was short.

The mill owner took over the responsibility previously held by the parish for keeping the children. Until 1802, there was no legislation setting out the mill owner's duties, and the treatment apprentices received depended on the type of man for whom they worked.

Robert Hyde Greg

'When there is no natural guardian, or, from circumstances, he is prevented from exercising his guardianship, and the law transfers to a master the privileges of a parent, amongst which is a command over the services of the child, it most properly imposes upon him also the *duties* of a parent, of providing the food, clothing and education of the child, and, as far as it can enforce the same, it ought to impose the duty of humanity and kind treatment.'
ROBERT HYDE GREG *The Factory Question, 1833.*

Mule Spinning c.1830.

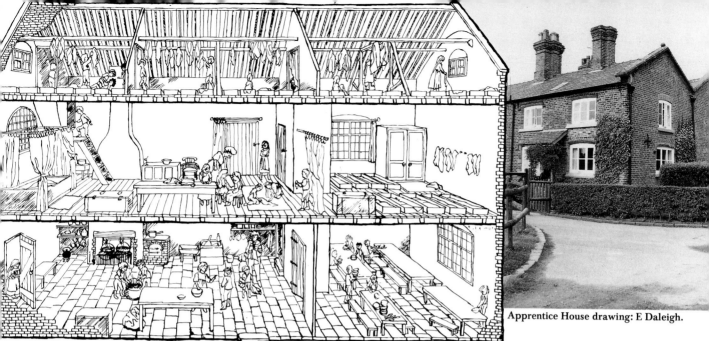

Apprentice House drawing: E Daleigh.

Life in the Apprentice House at Styal

The apprentices lived in the Apprentice House and were looked after by a superintendent and his wife. In addition to food and lodging, a doctor attended to their needs and some education was provided. The superintendents of the Apprentice House, George and Elizabeth Shawcross, gave this evidence to the Factory Commission in 1833:

How many children had you under your superintendance when you first came? Seventy-three when we first came and now sixty-seven; but we have had as many as ninety-seven . . . the average number is eighty-five.

How long do the children work in the mills? Twelve hours, from six in the morning to seven at night; an hour at noon for dinner, and half an hour at eight o'clock for breakfast: they always go out of the mill for their meals.

What are the terms on which they are taken? From nine to eighteen years of age: they are bound according to their ages when they come, generally nine years of age, but their apprenticeship never lasts after eighteen. They all live and eat in our house, and we take entire care of them.'

Joseph Sefton and Thomas Priestly were two apprentices who ran away from Styal.

'On Sunday we had for dinner boiled pork and potatoes. We also had peas, beans, turnips and cabbages in their season. Monday we had for dinner milk and bread and sometimes thick porridge. We always had as much as we could eat.
Tuesday we had milk and potatoes.
Wednesday sometimes bacon and potatoes sometimes milk and bread.
Thursday if we had bacon on Wednesday we had milk and bread.
Friday we used to have Lob Scouse (stew).
Saturday we used to dine on thick porridge.
We had only water to drink, when ill we were allowed tea.'

JOSEPH SEFTON, 1806

'Free' child labour was also employed. Such children, if not local, had to be housed in the village. They also had to be paid wages, and so were more expensive to employ. *'Free' means that the Gregs were free to dismiss them at any time.*

'We slept in long rooms, the girls on one side of the house and the boys on the other. There were a good many beds in each room and we had clean sheets oftener than once a month, our blankets and our rugs were perfectly clean, the rooms were whitewashed once a year, and were aired every day, we had clean shirts every Sunday, and new clothes when we wanted them.' THOMAS PRIESTLY, 1806

Recreation

'For their amusement, each has a small piece of garden: and in the playground a "weigh jolt" and a swing are fixed, and the ball and battledore were lying about.'

E W GRAY, *Notes and Observations written during a Ramble of Seven Weeks, 1843.*

Unhappy lot

The Styal apprentices appear to have lived better than many of their contemporaries. In towns in particular many apprentices lived and worked in appalling conditions.

'We went to our work at six in the morning without anything at all to eat or fire to warm us. For about a year after I went we never stopped for breakfast. The breakfast was brought to the mill in tin cans on large trays. It was milk, porridge and oat cake. They brought them into the room, and everyone took a tin and ate his breakfast as he could catch it, working away all the while. We stopt at twelve o'clock, and had an hour for dinner, but had the cleaning to do during that time. It took some of us half an hour to clean and oil the machinery. We went to dinner, which was potato-pie five days in the week.'

An apprentice from Cressbrook Mill

Quotations about apprentices lives

'. . . even at dead of night the machinery was never stopped, and when one set of fainting children were dragged from the mules another set were dragged from the reeking beds they were about to occupy, in order to take their places. The ventilation throughout the whole fabric was exceedingly imperfect; the heat, particularly in the room immediately beneath the roof was frightfully intense; cleanliness as to the beds, the floors, and the walls, utterly neglected; and even the persons of the children permitted to be filthy to excess, from having no soap allowed to assist their ablutions . . . .'
FRANCES TROLLOPE *The Life and Adventures of Michael Armstrong, The Factory Boy*, 1840.

'Our working hours were from 6 am in summer and in winter until 7 in the evening. There were no night workers although the boys did do overtime.
Our breakfasts were always brought to the mill . . . two days a week we had an hour allowed us for dinner.'
THOMAS PRIESTLY, 1806

'I was set the same as the others to attend two machines for spinning cotton, each of which spun 50 threads. My business was to supply these machines, to guide the threads occasionally and to twist them when they snapt . . . also I learned to take the machinery to pieces and apply the oil, a matter that required some care.' THOMAS PRIESTLY, 1806

'I was first employed to doff bobbins, that is taking a full bobbin off the spindles and putting an empty one on. I then sewed straps and put lists round the bundles. The straps turned the lists and the lists turned the wheels.'
JOSEPH SEFTON, 1806

Apprentices

From: The Life and Times of Michael Armstrong, 1840.

'In the first place, they are standing upon one leg, lifting up one knee, a great part of the day, keeping the ends up from the spindle; then there is the heat and dust; there are so many different forms of cruelty used upon them; then they are so liable to have their fingers catched and to suffer other accidents from the machinery; then the hours is so long, that I have seen them tumble down asleep amongst the straps and machinery, and so get cruelly hurt; then I would not have a child of mine there because there is not good morals; there is such a lot of them together that they learn mischief.'
ROBERT BLINCOE to the Factory Commission, 1833

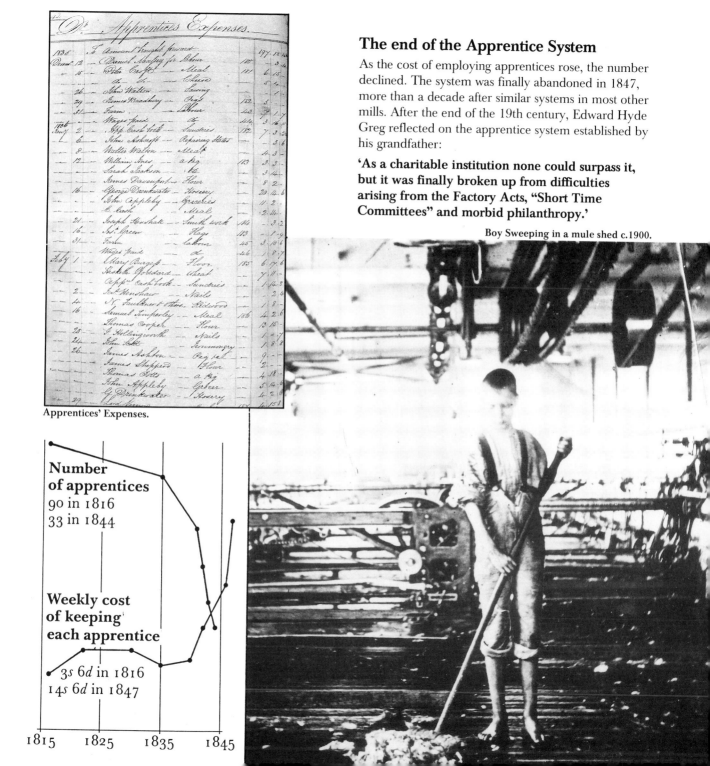

Apprentices' Expenses.

The end of the Apprentice System

As the cost of employing apprentices rose, the number declined. The system was finally abandoned in 1847, more than a decade after similar systems in most other mills. After the end of the 19th century, Edward Hyde Greg reflected on the apprentice system established by his grandfather:

'As a charitable institution none could surpass it, but it was finally broken up from difficulties arising from the Factory Acts, "Short Time Committees" and morbid philanthropy.'

Boy Sweeping in a mule shed c.1900.

Number of apprentices
90 in 1816
33 in 1844

Weekly cost of keeping each apprentice
3s 6d in 1816
14s 6d in 1847

1815   1825   1835   1845

Interior of a Workers Cottage in Styal, 1840s

The dimensions, layout and fittings of the reconstruction are taken directly from the ground floor rooms of one of Oak Cottages in Styal village.

Contemporary descriptions of Styal and other local sites have been used to establish a picture of a typical Styal cottage interior in the first half of the 19th century.

24

Religion

The Gregs and non-conformism

Many of the great entrepreneurs like the Gregs were non-conformists. As such they were restricted in what they could do: public office and the professions were closed to them. It may have been this, combined with their independent thinking, which turned them to commerce and aided their success.

Samuel Greg's wife Hannah was a member of the Unitarian Church. After marriage, he joined the Unitarian Cross Street Chapel in Manchester, where he met many prominent mill owners and merchants. The Gregs' children were brought up in this tradition; Robert Greg married another Unitarian, Mary Phillips.

Samuel Greg.

Hannah Greg.

Robert Peel

Richard Arkwright

Jedediah Strutt.

26

Religious life at Styal

Religion was at the centre of peoples' lives. It was natural for the Gregs to take an interest in the spiritual welfare of their workforce. The apprentice children went to Wilmslow church twice on Sundays (as required by the *Health and Morals of Apprentices* Act of 1802).

Samuel Greg built a chapel in Styal in 1822. In 1833, Robert Hyde Greg appointed as minister the Unitarian, the Rev John Colston, who made the chapel the centre of village life.

In the 1830s, a group of villagers formed a Methodist Society. In 1837, Robert Hyde Greg allowed an old shed to be converted into a Methodist Chapel.

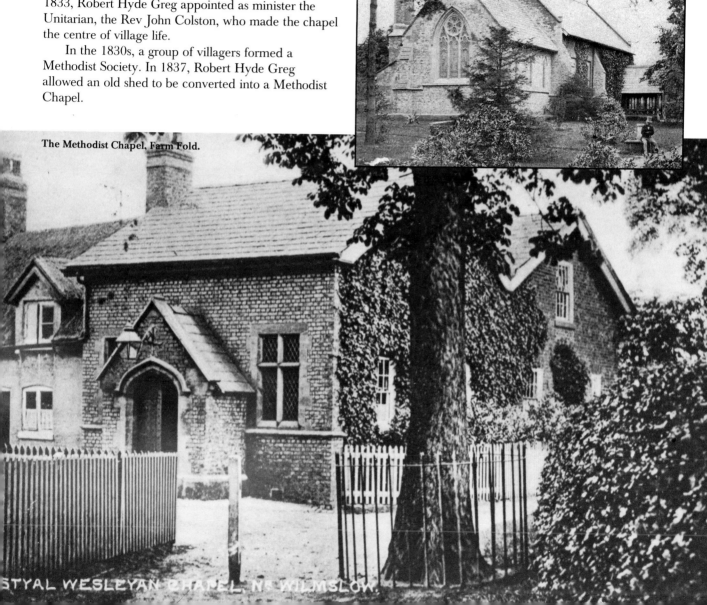

Norcliffe Chapel, with Robert Hyde Greg in the foreground.

The Methodist Chapel, Farm Fold.

STYAL WESLEYAN CHAPEL Nʳ WILMSLOW.

Education

'Education – without this you are nothing. You may possess all other things, and yet without this one you may be wanting everything.'
SAMUEL GREG JNR *The Condition of the Working Classes*, 1857.

In the mid 18th century, schools were only provided for privileged children. Mill owners like Samuel Greg were under no obligation to provide education for the children in their care until the *Health and Morals of Apprentices* Act came into force in 1802.

At Styal, Greg did provide education for the Mill's apprentice children: there is evidence that a succession of teachers was employed from 1788. Amongst the first was a music master (probably to teach dancing). School was on Sundays and, later, for a few hours after work as well.

Do you teach the children?—No; the ladies teach the girls, and the schoolmaster the boys, three nights a week, from eight to nine o'clock generally.

Then do you teach them nothing?—Sewing to the girls, who all make their own clothes and the shirts for the boys.

When do they find time for this work?—In the evening, after the mill stops.

Are they never too tired to work at the needlework?—No; they are much more tired when they have a play-day, on the mill stopping; they want to go to bed much sooner on those days.

When do the ladies teach the girls?—Sunday afternoon; and then there is a schoolmistress besides, who teaches them at the same time; they have also a monitress to a certain number of girls, who hears her class every other evening.

Can all the apprentices read and write?—Not all: the boys can, but the girls have not so much time, as they must mind the sewing; they can all read very well, and most write a little, but not so much as the boys.

When they are past eighteen, do they generally remain in the mill?—Yes; and go out to lodgings or their friends.

Evidence given to 1833 Factory Commission by Mr and Mrs Shawcross, Superintendents of the Apprentice House.

Gradually the curriculum expanded – mathematics became part of the syllabus as well as reading and writing.

Oak School children c1900.

Oak School

In 1823, the Gregs built Oak School which the village children could also attend. Young children were taught during the day, the older ones at night. The apprentices attended one night a week in classes of eight.

Mutual improvement

In the 1830s, a Mutual Improvement Society was formed for the adult men in the village. The Gregs' sons sometimes gave lectures at their meetings.

'I am now very busy reading and arranging and meditating for my lecture on history which will be ten times the labour of my last; also collecting from all history and all science every fact or principal, or opinion, or admission, or event which can in any way bear upon magnetism . . . which I think will astonish the natives when I bring it forward.'

Letter from W R GREG *to his sister,* 1830

It is possible that John Venables learnt to read through this society. By the time of his second marriage, he could sign his name.

Many manufacturers felt they needed workers with some education for the new industries to succeed. In 1841 Samuel Greg Jnr described the value of education for the working classes:

'In all plans for the education of the labouring classes my object would be not to raise any individuals amongst them above their condition, but to elevate the condition itself.'

Oak School.

Half time scholars at Styal, 1847.

The 'half time' system was introduced in 1844. This meant that children under the age of 13 were restricted to 6½ hours of work a day with three hours at school, or 5 hours at school on three alternate days.

29

Health at Styal

The factory doctor

Samuel Greg employed Dr Holland of Knutsford from 1788 for a fee of £20 a year. He was one of the earliest factory doctors and was responsible for the health of the apprentices. Most of the records of his weekly visits survive.

One task was to examine new apprentices. They were given a month's probation to check on their health and strength.

Pre-employment examination of 292 children at Quarry Bank Mill, 1811–1842

203 healthy
 32 delicate
 28 inflammation of the eyes
  7 enlarged glands
  4 scrofulous
  4 under age
  3 old injuries
  1 scurvy
  1 bedwetter
  1 weak intellect
  1 dwarvish
  1 weak ankle
  1 unhealthy
  4 feverish (1 scarlet fever)

Dr Peter Holland.

From the Doctor's notebook

Transcription of the above:

Oct. 13
Margaret Badding
To take the medicine
according to the directions –
if the pain in the chest is
not better on Sunday, to have
six leeches applied to the
most painful part – and if
it still continues to apply
a blister – to take no meals
and to drink freely of weak
tea, barley water or toast and water.

Leeches and white powders . . .

Dr Holland's prescription book shows the types of illnesses he treated and the remedies he provided. Most of the treatments prescribed were as effective as any known at that time.

Self-help: the Sick Club

Samuel Greg provided loans to establish other medical facilities including a dispensary, a Sick Club, and a Female Society (1827) to assist with the problems of childbirth.

Membership of the Sick Club was compulsory: a farthing (¼d) was taken off each shilling of their wages. The club paid out up to twelve weeks half pay for illnesses and fixed expenses for funerals:

Child . . . . . 3 shillings,
Adult . . . . . 5 shillings,
Head of family . . . 8 shillings.

Life and death

Life expectancy was better in Styal than in the towns. In 1837, R. H. Greg estimated the mortality rates of his employees as 7 per 1,000. This compares favourably to 33 per 1,000 in Manchester. The mortality rate is the number out of the total workforce who died in a year.

C Turner Thackrah, the 'father' of occupational health, watched the workers leaving a factory in Oxford Road, Manchester in 1832:

Operatives leaving Manchester cotton mills.

'I stood . . . and observed the streams of operatives as they left the mill. The children were ill-looking, small, sickly, barefoot and ill-clad. The men were as pallid and thin as the children. The women were most respectable, though not a fresh face amongst them caught my eye . . . there I saw a degenerate race, stunted and enfeebled – children that were never to be healthy adults.'

By comparison the people of Styal were healthy. Although they also suffered from the heat, dust and noise of the mill they were cared for by a doctor and the rural environment and housing conditions were in their favour.

Rules of Styal Sick Club.

Albion Mills on fire.

Accidents and Safety

The new cotton mills were full of people unfamiliar with the machinery, working long hours. This situation produced great new risks of injury and fire.

Quarry Bank Mill seems to have had a reasonable safety record. In 1833 Samuel Greg told the Factory Commission that his machinery was fenced off. This was not made compulsory until 1844.

The same Commissioners asked the Shawcrosses (superintendants of the Apprentice House):

'Can you say how many deaths have occurred among the apprentices in the twenty-two years you have been here?'

They replied: 'Seventeen deaths, only one of whom was killed by an accident at the machinery: it was his own play, not in the factory, but in the wheel race; it was in the place where the water wheel was putting up.'

In spite of precautions taken at the mill, accidents did happen – particularly towards the end of a working day:

'I've getten no head for numbers, but this I know, that *by far th' greater part o' the accidents as comed in, happened in th' last two hours o' work,* when folk getten tired and careless. The surgeon said it were all true, and that he were going to bring that fact to light.'

ELIZABETH GASKELL *Mary Barton,* 1848.

Accidents at Quarry Bank Mill

Apprentices were often injured because their work involved going under the machines – the loss of fingers was common.

'. . . there was a great deal of cotton in the machine, one of the wheels caught my finger and tore it off, it was the forefinger of my left hand. I was attended by the surgeon of the factory Mr Holland and in about six weeks I recovered.'

THOMAS PRIESTLY to Middlesex magistrates, 1806

Accidents that occurred were recorded in the Mill Memoranda:

'On the 23rd June 1845 an accident resulting fatally happened to a weaving overlooker's assistant named Joseph Davenport, some 25 years of age. While engaged in doing some job about a loom, the buckle of a strap caught his shirt sleeve and snatched him up to the drum, and wrenched his arm off at the shoulder. He was immediately removed to the Manchester Infirmary where he died after lingering a few days.'

Mill Memoranda, 1845

'On the 6th of March 1865 a very melancholy accident befell a lad named John Foden, about 13 years of age. While engaged sweeping under a Mule his head was caught between the Roller Beam and the carriage as the latter was putting up – and completely smashed, death being instantaneous.'

Mill Memoranda, 1865

John Venables, a mechanic, was reputedly killed in an accident at the mill in 1865. The story is told by his descendants, though there is no record in the Mill Memoranda.

The campaign for safety begins

Accidents were an accepted part of industrial life. They became so frequent in cotton mills that steps had to be taken. In 1833, following a Factory Commission Report, the government established the Factory Inspectorate. The purpose of this body was to regulate working conditions in cotton mills and so reduce the risk of injury to workers. Yet progress was slow: twenty years later, Charles Dickens was campaigning in the journal *Household Words* for tighter laws and more men to enforce them.

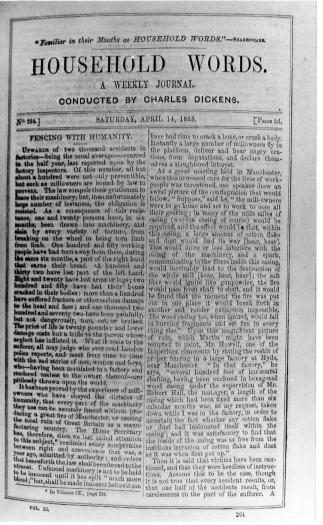

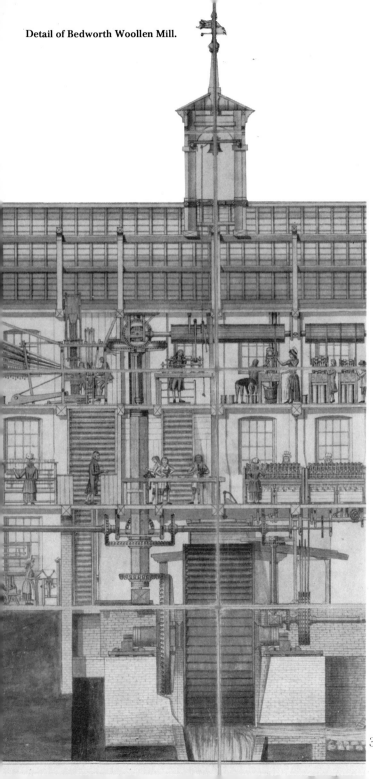

Detail of Bedworth Woollen Mill.

Working Conditions

'While the engine runs people must work – men, women, and children are yoked together with iron and steam.' DR J P KAY, 1832.

When Samuel Greg built Quarry Bank Mill, the idea of factories was new. Until this time, cotton had been spun and woven in cottages or workshops by small groups of workmen and their families.

Domestic Spinning

In the new cotton mills, workers were grouped together in large numbers. The waterwheel, the rhythm of the machines and the factory clock set the pace. At first, this imposed discipline was unfamiliar and much disliked and feared.

Domestic industry in the 18th century.

Dean Mills, Bolton.

34

The Working Day at Styal, c.1830

5.30 am	The day's work begins.
8.30 am	Break of 10 minutes for breakfast.
1.00 pm	30 minutes for dinner – hasten home to the village and back.
5.30 pm	Tea at the machines.
8.00 pm	End of the working day – unless overtime is demanded.

A FRYER *Wilmslow Graves,* 1835

Work in the mills was often monotonous and repetitive; a child could spend all day tying ends of cotton or cleaning fluff from the machines.

The Gregs, unlike other mill owners, operated only one shift. It was a long one, however: 13 hours a day before 1847. In summer, when the river was too low for a full day's production, hours were shorter. The time had to be made up with longer hours in the winter.

Robert Hyde Greg opposed the campaign in the 1840s for a shorter working day (the Ten Hours Movement) on the grounds that: shorter hours would lower production; workers' wages would be reduced; foreign competition would be given an unfair advantage, and mills powered by water needed to have a flexible system of work to make up for hours lost due to drought.

Mill Girls c.1900.

'THE FACTORY GIRL.

DEDICATED TO JOHN WOOD, ESQ.,

BY ROBERT DIBB, DEWSBURY.

Who is she with pallid face?
That slowly moves with languid pace,
Her limbs bespeak her wearied frame
She seems in suff'ring, grief, and pain!
" A little child"—with list'ning ear,
Approach'd me with a falling tear
    And said—'tis Jane the Factory Girl!

I took her by her little hand—
Though from fatigue, she scarce could stand,
I tried to soothe her tender grief
By friendship's pow'r to give relief;
And ask'd in accents most sincere
What caus'd the anguish so severe?
    Of Jane—the Village Factory Girl!

She answer'd!—near that little wood,
Once liv'd my mother—kind—and good:
My father died upon that morn,
When I unhappily was born:
And now one only sister dear
Is left—the broken heart to cheer
    Of Jane—the Orphan Factory Girl!

Oh! Sir! we work from morning's light
Till darkness settles at the night:
No rest we know—no parents come
To welcome our return to home,
We call on Heaven to bless our cot
For earthly friends have all forgot
    The poor neglected Factory Girl!

The overlooker—many a time,
Without a fault—without a crime,
Has beat me with such savage might
That scarce could I reach home at night:
Oh! then I've wept in anguish deep,
And blest those parents now asleep
    Who lov'd poor Jane, the Factory Girl!

Oh! yes! upon their lowly bier
Oft have I shed a mournful tear!
And wish'd that I alas could sleep
No more to suffer, nor to weep:
But soon I feel that welcome death
Will claim the last—the parting breath
    Of Jane, the wretched Factory Girl!

She cast her eyes with wildness round,
Then sunk exhausted on the ground;
I clasp'd the sufferer to my breast,
But she—poor girl—was now at rest!!
No cruel tyrant now could place
A tear upon the snowy face
    Of Jane, the lifeless Factory Girl!

Ye! who alone on Gold are bent,
Blush! at the Murder'd Innocent,
Let not Old England's glorious pride
Be stain'd by black Infanticide!!
But let Humanity's bright Ray
Protect from greedy Tyrant's sway
    The poor defenceless Factory Girl!

PRICE 1d.—*The profits arising therefrom to go towards forwarding the*
TEN HOURS BILL!!!

E. WILLAN, PRINTER, DEWSBURY.

When Quarry Bank Mill went into production, there were no regulations governing working conditions in factories.

The hazards of working in a cotton mill gradually became apparent to the medical profession. Listed below are some common occupational health risks and their principal causes.

Eye inflamation from the use of tallow and Argand lamps.

Lung disease (byssinosis) from breathing-in cotton dust in badly-ventilated rooms.

Deafness from long exposure to noisy machinery.

'Mule-spinners' cancer' (cancer of the groin) from the oil on the mule spindles.

Cancer of the mouth and **tuberculosis** from 'kissing the shuttle'.

Body deformities from constant bending, and lack of exercise when young.

The air in the cotton mills had to be kept hot and humid so that the thread would not break in the machines. At Quarry Bank Mill the rooms were kept at a temperature of 64° to 70°F.

There are many reports of terrible conditions in the early cotton mills. Observers complained of the smell, the heat, the lack of sanitation and the dust, the ill-treatment of workers and the long hours. It fell to the Factory Commission to examine these claims.

Is there any distinct or specific provision for the ventilation of your factory, if there is any such provision, describe its nature and effects?
In scutching (cleaning the cotton), the dust and flock is carried off through flues by means of powerful fans, leaving the room perfectly free from inconvenience.

State whether the provision depends on the opening of windows, or other casual means?
Yes, every window opening at the top.

Is the ventilation regulated by the foremen, or overlooker or manufacturer, or is it controlled at the discretion of all, or of any of the persons employed?
By the overlooker.

Have you any arrangements in your manufactory for the health or convenience of the workpeople, such as arrangements to enable them to change their clothes on entering the manufactory, or for washing or putting on additional clothing on leaving the manufactory, or any arrangements to ensure the personal cleanliness of those employed thereat; if you have, specify those arrangements, and the date of their introduction.
No dressing rooms. They seldom change other than their cloaks, shawls and bonnets; these they hang up on pegs within the rooms. Many put on pinafores or aprons, and have slippers to work in. All are required to come clean. Can wash their hands. It is a clean employment.

SAMUEL GREG to the Factory Commissioners, 1833

'Kissing the shuttle.'

'My legs are now as bent as you see. *(The knees are bent dreadfully, both inwards and forwards. The height of the boy, who is fifteen, is three feet nine inches.)* Got my knees bent with standing so long. Remember when my knees began to fail me; I had been at the mill not two years; it was at Anderson's; my knees hurt me very bad then: when we tired, you know, there was nought to sit on; I was obliged to lay hold of someat to keep me up; it used to be very bad towards night; sometimes very sleepy; we used to get thumped sometimes by the overlooker, who was a woman . . . .'

WILLIAM PICKLES of Ward's Mill, Bradford, to the Factory Commissioners, 1833.

'The bad effects of the cotton business have already appeared in the pale sallow complexions of the people in it and some young tender constitutions have already fallen a sacrifice to it. Whether this is to be attributed to some pernicious effluvia arising from the wool, or the smaller fussy particles of it flying about during their work and drawn into the lungs by respiration, or the attitude or action of the spinner who is obliged to lean upon his breast or stomach, or the close confinement in crowded rooms where they suck in corrupted putrid air, or as in such numbers of men and women assembled together in this employment.'

S FINNEY *A Historical Survey of the Parish of Wilmslow,* 1787

'The ceaseless whirring of a million hissing wheels, seizes on the tortured ear; and while threatening to destroy the delicate sense, seems bent on proving first, with a sort of mocking mercy, of how much suffering it can be the cause. The scents that reek around, from oil, tainted water, and human filth, with that last worst nausea, arising from the hot refuse of atmospheric air, left by some hundred pairs of labouring lungs, render the act of breathing a process of difficulty, disgust and pain. But what the eye brings home to the heart of those, who look round upon the horrid earthly hell, is enough to make it all forgotten; for who can think of villainous smells, or heed the suffering of the ear-wracking sounds, while they look upon hundreds of helpless children, divested of every trace of health, of joyousness, and even of youth!'

FRANCES TROLLOPE *The Life and Adventures of Michael Armstrong the Factory Boy,* 1840

From: The Life and Times of Michael Armstrong, 1840.

Labour Relations

A loyal workforce

At Styal, the workforce seem to have remained loyal to the Gregs, even during the slump in trade in the 1840s and in periods of general unrest.

The recognition of Trade Unions

During the mid-19th century, skilled Trade Unions gradually became recognised, and with the Acts of 1871 and 1875, their legal position was established.

The struggles of the early Unions

Early trade unions were local and confined to one craft because of the common problems of the workers in that craft. In 1799, the Combination Acts were passed. They aimed to prevent workmen joining together. The Government's decision was influenced by fear of a revolution similar to that of France.

The first two decades of the 19th century saw the development of a movement for workers' rights. The North of England also saw violent resistance to the introduction of new machinery. Fruitless strikes, rioting and machine breaking (the Luddite Rebellion) took place.

Satirical cartoon, 1840

Raiding the Workhouse, Stockport, 1842.

The 'Peterloo Massacre' in St Peter's Field, Manchester, 1819.

Cotton operatives clashing with the military in Preston, 1842.

'A fair day's pay!'

'A fair day's pay for a fair day's labour!'

Labour relations at Styal seem to have been good. There is little evidence of trade union activity and there are no records of strikes until the 20th century. There were some disagreements, however:

When members of the Short Time committee visited Styal in 1842 to encourage the workers to strike, 'few left' to join the strikers. Those that did 'were generally glad enough to return, except one or two of bad character.'

'We have had many disputes regarding wages and some upon discipline, but in our whole experience we never had one respecting hours of labour.'

R H GREG, to the Factory Commission, 1833

'We have (August 1842) to record' the disastrous occurrence of a turn-out of the manufacturing labourers in and about Manchester . . . the sudden and turbulent display of congregated thousands, leaving their daily employment – marching upon mills, forcing willing and unwilling alike to join them and, in a moment, paralysing the whole activity of the natural enterprise of their neighbourhood, – arose, in the first instance, from a reduction in wages in one quarter, given almost without notice, and taken by the men as the omen of a general intention on the part of the masters everywhere else.'

Illustrated London News

'During the operative disturbances of this year the "Turnouts" visited Quarry Bank on the 11th August. On their approach the Mill was stopped and remained standing for the 3 following weeks. All able-bodied men were sworn in as special constables and patrolled the neighbourhood by night and day for most of that time. Comparatively little damage was done at the Mill, the mob moving on to Wilmslow and from thence to Bollington and not returning in this direction.'

G H GREG, *Mill Memoranda*, 1842

AMALGAMATED ASSOCIATION OF CARD & BLOWING ROOM OPERATIVES

ESTD 1886

This is to Certify

that   was admitted a Member of

          District of this Amalgamated Society on the

day of   18

District Secretary   Wm Mulliner General Secretary

Union Certificate.

Discipline at Styal

'The new virtues that the workers were persuaded to adopt were those requisite for a material civilisation: regularity, punctuality, obedience, thrift, providence, sobriety and industry.'
S D CHAPMAN, J D CHAMBERS, *The Beginnings of Industrial Britain*, 1970.

Mill owners saw the benefit of strict discipline, and workers were summoned by the bell.

Fines and Punishments

The routine and order of mill life had to be enforced. At Styal, a system of deterrents encouraged co-operation. These were usually in the form of fines which were paid by the children working overtime. Each offence had its price – a heavy one for apprentices earning only a few pennies a week:

Stealing apples 5s
Breaking windows 2s 6d

A serious offence was to run away. This caused mill owners great inconvenience. The fine was 8d per day plus expenses – any money spent on their location and return.

In 1836, two ten-year-old girls ran away. Lucy Garner returned after four days, Esther Price after a week. They were threatened with having their hair cut off, but after a consultation with local magistrates, they were confined for a period matching their absence. A fine was also imposed. This harsh treatment brought criticism from the Factory Inspectorate.

Robert Hyde Greg gave this account of the circumstance connected with the punishment of Esther Price and Lucy Garner:

'. . . The windows (were) boarded, partly to prevent communication from without, partly to prevent her escape. The room was partially dark. Her food; milk porridge and bread morning and evening was the same as the other girls, but no dinner.'

The Clock Tower, Styal.

44

Discipline at other mills

Punishments at Styal were light compared to the more brutal methods used to enforce discipline at other mills. Beatings were common, and sometimes vices or weights were attached to the nose and ears.

The memoirs of Robert Blincoe, published in 1832, describe the horrors of life in some mills. 'Mr Needham (Master, Litton Mill, Derbyshire) stands accused of having been in the habit of knocking down apprentices with his clenched fists — kicking them about when down, beating them to excess with sticks, or flogging them with horse-whips; of seizing them by the ears, lifting them from the ground and forcibly dashing them down on the floor, pinching them 'till his nails met! Blinco declares his oppressors used to seize him by the hair of his head and tear it off by a handful at a time, 'till the crown of his head had become as bald as the back of his hand.'

Weaver wearing ear weights and nose clamp.

George Cruickshank's view of life in the mills.

A settled Community

Industrialisation often brought social problems in its wake. For the city worker poor conditions at work often matched squalor and overcrowding in the home.

At Styal the site and layout of the village and its institutions provided a base for a settled community.

In the mill itself conditions, though harsh by modern standards, were perhaps better than those found in other factories.

Relations between master and workforce seem to have been good. Beyond this the Greg family influenced all aspects of their workers' lives and shaped the community in which they lived.

Two hundred years after its foundation Styal still provides an unspoilt example of a factory community, the surviving buildings reflecting earlier social ties.

Mill mechanics c.1890.